Book of Encouragement-Journal
Volume 1

By

Sisters Anointed for Encouragement, Inc. (SAFE Encouragement)

To request permissions, contact the publisher at
S.A.F.E.Inc@safeencouragement.com

Hardcover: ISBN;978-1-7923-5599-8
Paperback: ISBN;978-1-7923-5599-8
Audiobook: ISBN;978-1-7923-5599-8
Library of Congress Number: TXu2-229-947 2020
First paperback edition: January 2021
Edited by: Badia Atcherson; Monica Dorsey; Juan L. Smith, and Algie Atcherson

Layout by: Juan L. Smith

Photographs by :AESI Photography http://www.aesiphotography.com/
Tara Pollard Smith (Photographer)
Printed by: Book Baby Publishers
Publisher: Safe Encouragement, 1201 Shady Glen Dr.
Forestville, MD 20747
www.safeencouragement.com

All Scripture quotations, unless otherwise indicated, are taken from the Holy Bible, (KJV; NIV, and/or ESV)

IN MEMORY OF

April Renee' Smith-Joyner
December 5, 1975-September 8, 2008

The Ultimate, daughter, sister, wife, mother, relative, friend and life coach. Before her death, and with a bachelor's degree in Sociology, she founded "DREAMS" (Dedicated to Rejuvenating, Empowering and Achieving Meaningful Success). Many individuals (married and single) were blessed with the life skills April provided in her positive, uplifting motivating, and fully spirited retreats and individual coaching sessions.

"Living your dreams are worth it and more importantly you are worth living your dreams"
April Joyner

FORWARD

Our Vision is to reach men, women and families through prayer and Gods word. Around the world, to be the voice to the silenced, and to encourage them to overcome their struggles, adversities, obstacles, trials, and tribulations.

"Then the eleven disciples went to Galilee, to the mountain where Jesus had told them to go. When they saw him, they worshiped him; but some doubted. Then Jesus came to them and said, all authority in heaven and on earth has been given to me. Therefore, go and make disciples of all nations, baptizing them in the name of the Father and of the Son and of the Holy Spirit, and teaching them to obey everything I have commanded you. And surely, I am with you always, to the very end of the age"
(Matthew 28:16-20).

The following collections are from our daily devotions as published on our webpage www.safeencouragement.com

TABLE OF CONTENTS

From the Heart and Spirit of Sister Badia A.

Getting Rid of the Mess, Making Room for the New

Rise and Shine! God, we give you all the glory and honor for you are worthy to be praised! In Jesus name,

AMEN!

In life, most of us become excited about change, and the newness it can bring. The change we go through can cause us to get rid of some things(s). Before we can walk in a new direction, some things are forced to end. Some of the things we rid ourselves of maybe refreshing and eventually become rewarding, whereas other things may be difficult to let go.

The process of getting rid of the redundant mess can strengthen us with passion and strength needed to heal from the loss of the thing(s) we needed to get rid of. The entire process is a part of God's plan. We are to walk in purpose on the assigned path He created.

Think about the things we said goodbye to as we prepared ourselves to welcome in the new. Most of the thing (s) were probably in our lives because WE allowed them. Somethings that we let go purposefully may have been to get us to a place of understanding; understanding who we are in Christ and in our personal lives. When the door closed, another door opened. Doors revealing new gifts and assignments that we never thought were ours. Can you imagine still being in the cleared space of yesterday, and never getting the chance to see what a new day can bring?

Encouragement/ Prayer:
Our father's plan is for us to experience the fullness of ALL He has for us. It is our job, as His children, to be open and ready to receive All His abundant blessings given to us. We would slight ourselves if we made the choice based on familiar feelings and experiences. Experiences that may cause us to stay in bondage with yesterday's mess. It is our best advantage, if we allow the old door to shut, leaving space for the newly assigned door to open.

My prayer is for us to have faith in the new. Whatever our new is, allow the Lord to equip us with the ability(s) to do some awesome things in His name. Your assignment(s) is created just for you. You can and will fulfill them, In Jesus name, AMEN!

Ephesians 4:17-24 English Standard Version (ESV)

The New Life
Now, this I say and testify in the Lord, that you must no longer walk as the Gentiles do, in the futility of their minds. They are darkened in their understanding, alienated from the life of God because of the ignorance that is in them, due to their hardness of heart. They have become callous and have given themselves up to sensuality, greedy to practice every kind of impurity. But that is not the way you learned Christ!—assuming that you have heard about him and were taught in him, as the truth is in Jesus, to put off your old self, which belongs to your former manner of life and is corrupt through deceitful desires, and to be renewed in the spirit of your minds, and to put on the new self, created after the likeness of God in true righteousness and holiness.

Journal

| |
| |
| |
| |
| |
| |
| |
| |
| |
| |
| |
| |

From the Heart and Spirit of Sister Monica D.

From the Heart and Spirit of Sister Monica D.

Good day, Great day Everyone!

Lord because of You, I am blessed to see this day. May You be my guidance and instruct my path for your glory. In Jesus name, Amen.

The Assignment Will Be Completed

In the beginning, God created man, Adam.

(Gen. 2:20-,22). But for Adam no suitable helper was found. So, the Lord God caused man to fall into a deep sleep; and while he was sleeping, he took one of the man's ribs and then closed up the place with flesh. Then the Lord God made a woman from the rib, He had taken out of the man and he brought her to the man.

One day a serpent came to her, deceived her, and led her to believe that God's word was not actually what it was. She believed the serpent above God and by this deceived God and her eyes were opened to the world. Even though she went against God, He forgave her and Adam but consequences to her lack of faith caused her to find God's victory another way. Her disobedience led them to suffer the consequences of being disobedient. God's assignment to Adam and Eve was not the lesson to not eat from the tree in the garden. No, that was an instruction from God. The assignment, Hallelujah was....to be fruitful in mankind and make many nations in which we are here today as a testimony of God's assignment to them.

God's assignment for you is part of His divine plan for your life. Follow the assignment. Don't look back, move forward. Get excited about your future in God. And if you make a mistake, if you sin, remember God is a forgiving God and His promises never change.

Difficulty cannot keep you from your purpose. In God's assignment we will face some difficulty, but that is when God can show us his full potential and His power. And all will witness His glory in your life. Just remain faithful.

The enemy cannot break the circle of protection that God has around us. If God brings you to it, he will bring you through it. And your assignment will be completed.

Be Blessed, And Always Pray!

Journal

Sister Juan Sharing HER(s)tory today. Just a song and a few words from the Lord.

Are you praising the Lord during your circumstances and situations?

Take a moment, (or more), and look around. 2017 is gone. 2018 is bringing it on. Say 'THANK YOU LORD". Your "THANK YOU LORD" may be (I believe it will be) the words that change the course of your time in 2018. Just a thought.....

May you be encouraged by the lyrics of a song by the Mighty Clouds of Joy, and the verses of scripture from the Word of the Lord.

LYRICS-EVERYBODY OUGHT TO PRAISE HIS NAME:

Oh, I woke up early this morning my heart was beating right on time. I said Lord I truly thank you for opening' up these eyes of mine. Then I went over to my window. And, while looking through the shade Once again I had to tell him Thank -You –Lord For letting' me see another day. Now the sun was brightly shining. The wind was blowing' not too strong. In a treehouse just a few feet away Little Robin sang his song. I don't know what he was singing. Pretty soon he was on his way. Who can say he wasn't being Grateful. And saying thank you for another day. (Everybody ought to) Praise His name; (Be thankful and) Praise His name

(Everybody ought to) Praise His name; (Cause if the robin can say Thank You), You can do it too!!!

SCRIPTURES:

Numbers 6:22-27 (NIV) The Priestly Blessing the LORD said to Moses, "Tell Aaron and his sons, 'This is how you are to bless the Israelites. Say to them: """The LORD bless you and keep you; the LORD make his face shine on you and be gracious to you; the LORD turn his face toward you and give you peace."'" "So, they will put my name on the Israelites, and I will bless them."

Psalm 16:7 (NIV) I will praise the LORD, who counsels me; even at night my heart instructs me.

Psalm 34:1-4 (NIV) Of David. When he pretended to be insane before Abimelek, who drove him away, and he left. I will extol the LORD at all times; his praise will always be on my lips. I will glory in the LORD; let the afflicted hear and rejoice. Glorify the LORD with me; let us exalt his name together. I sought the LORD, and he answered me; he delivered me from all my fears.

Psalm 28:7 (NIV) The LORD is my strength and my shield; my heart trusts in him, and he helps me. My heart leaps for joy, and with my song I praise him.

Psalm 147:1-6 (NIV) Praise the LORD. How good it is to sing praises to our God, how pleasant and fitting to praise him! The LORD builds up Jerusalem; he gathers the exiles of Israel. He heals the brokenhearted and binds up their wounds. He determines the number of the stars and calls them each by name. Great is our Lord and mighty in power; his understanding has no limit. The LORD sustains the humble but casts the wicked to the ground.

EVERYBODY OUGHT TO PRAISE HIM!!!

Now may the Love of God be with you, the peace of Jesus maintain you and the Holy Spirit restrain you. In Jesus Name and For His Sake. Can I get an "AMEN" "AMEN" "AMEN

Journal

Hello, Everyone, this is your sister Algie. Praying for our obedience in following the Assignments that God has before us!

If you pay close attention you will see in the Bible that Abraham had an assignment from God. He was told to

15

leave his family and go wherever God lead him. Mary's assignment was to birth Jesus. Where would we if they did not listen?

Can you imagine the consequences when we do not obey what God tells us?

As a young child, I remember looking out of my window talking to God, knowing the bond that we were forming. It's funny I say we. But in my mind, God and I have this connection that was formed on that day. He told me the type of person I would become, and I agreed. I thought ... I like that person, caring, considerate, nice to my friends. You see He spoke to me in a manner that a child could understand. I remember a time in my life when I thought I could steal something. Of course, I got caught, and gave it back before I even left the store. I ran home so fast, not on the main street, I ran through alley. I was so scared the police would catch me and put me in jail. For months, I was haunted by that episode. To this day I think of it when I drive near the street where the store is. The lesson I learned, of course, thou shall not steal. That, incident, among others, taught me lessons I carried with me now, as an adult. Thinking of the effect of stealing - how it made me feel as a person, taking what does not belong to me.

Now I've left my Assignment, taking me to a dark place that I will never travel again. STEALING REALLY! The good news is that God will use our failures for His purposes. I changed for the better. All of that has changed me for the better. God's Assignments caused me to become a better person. Most times in our lives, our mistakes can make us stronger people. If we don't learn

16

anything else, we will know what we should not do. Look at what you can learn from your detours. Like driving, I didn't know those houses were back there. It's what we do with our lives that makes us who we are. And, who we become.

God is omnipotent. He is the Great I Am over this world. It is His nature. All through history, people were given God-sized assignments for the express purpose of delivering His word, advancing His kingdom, and revealing His Divine Glory and Power.

If God came to you and gave you an assignment, how would you respond?

What would be your reaction to His assignment?

Let me give you some help on the subject...

There are things that you probably don't like right?

Assignment: Change it

There are people that need assistance.

Assignment: Help them

All Creation is designed to solve problems.

I am a braider, weaver. So, you need to change your look, I got you.

Dentist can solve teeth problems

Mothers can solve your emotional issues and change your diaper.

lawyers, mechanics.......

Jeremiah 29:11 says: "I know what I have planned for you", says the Lord. "I have good plans for you, not plans to hurt you. I will give you a hope and a future. Then you will call my name. You will come to me and pray to me, and I will listen to you. You will search for me. And when you search for me with all your heart, you will find me! I will let you find me," says the Lod. "And I will bring you back from your captivity."

I love you. I hope I have inspired you to live your best life. In Jesus Name and for His sake Amen!

We cannot complete our assignments without first professing our belief in our Savior. Then we must accept and trust the journey. We must be encouraged to understand that sole purpose for us to have the faith and trust we have, is all to grow closer to our Father. The assignment(s) will never become overwhelming when we choose to walk with Christ and not without Him. We will be amazed at the number of things we can accomplish when we make the decision to conjoin our faith and trust together...

Encouragement/Prayer
Joshua 1:9 English Standard Version (ESV)
Have I not commanded you? Be strong and courageous. Do not be frightened, and do not be dismayed, for the LORD your God is with you wherever you go."

2 Samuel 7:28 English Standard Version (ESV)
And now, O Lord GOD, you are God, and your words are true, and you have promised this good thing to your servant.

Proverbs 3:5-7 English Standard Version (ESV)
Trust in the LORD with all your heart, and do not lean on

your own understanding. In all your ways acknowledge him, and he will make straight your paths. Be not wise in your own eyes; fear the LORD and turn away from evil.

Journal

From the Heart and Spirit of Sister Badia A.

Good Monday Morning to you!

FAITH.... AND.... TRUST.... YOU CAN'T HAVE ONE WITHOUT THE OTHER

Rise and Shine! God, we give you all the glory and honor for you are worthy to be praised! In Jesus name, AMEN!

It is my opinion that faith and trust cannot be separated.

How can you trust something or someone you do not have faith in?

As we continue to journey in our assignment(s), the next step is for us to strengthen our faith in God. Trust our designated process. As believers, it is important for us to have faith and trust in God's purpose for creating us. It can be exceedingly difficult to verbally decide to trust our journey without believing in the one who created it.

When such decisions are made, it can cause mental malfunctions to take place, leading us on a path of wrong choices. The wrong choices we make can be relational, with both people, and God. If our faith in God is not concrete, our trust in Him will be weakened by our view of who God is in us and to the world. If we believe that God is the creator of all things, we should trust in Him and the power, through us, He possesses to assign, direct, and birth some magnificent things.

When it comes to our assigned journeys, we need both to

help us learn the who, what, when, where, and how's. We read throughout the Bible and learn about the numerous times God blessed those he chose to use. He chose them because of the belief and trust they had in Him.

We cannot complete our assignments without first professing our belief in our Savior. Then we must accept and trust the journey. We must be encouraged to understand that sole purpose for us to have the faith and trust we have, is all to grow closer to our Father. The assignment(s) will never become overwhelming when we choose to walk with Christ and not without Him. We will be amazed at the number of things we can accomplish when we make the decision to conjoin our faith and trust together...

Encouragement/Prayer
Joshua 1:9 English Standard Version (ESV)
Have I not commanded you? Be strong and courageous. Do not be frightened, and do not be dismayed, for the LORD your God is with you wherever you go."

2 Samuel 7:28 English Standard Version (ESV)
And now, O Lord GOD, you are God, and your words are true, and you have promised this good thing to your servant.

Proverbs 3:5-7 English Standard Version (ESV)
Trust in the LORD with all your heart, and do not lean on your own understanding. In all your ways acknowledge him, and he will make straight your paths. Be not wise in your own eyes; fear the LORD and turn away from evil.

Journal

From the Heart and Spirit of Sister Monica D.

Good Morning Everyone!!

Lord we give thanks to You today for the blessing of waking us up this morning, starting us on our way, and for the giving of your grace and mercy to see us throughout this day. In Jesus name, Amen!!

Scripture:
Psalm 34:17-19 (NIV)
17 The righteous cry out, and the Lord hears them; he delivers them from all their troubles.
18 The Lord is close to the brokenhearted and saves those who are crushed in spirit. 19 The righteous person may have many troubles, but the Lord delivers him from them all;

The Lord hears and answers prayers. In our time of need, we should know to turn to God for guidance and understanding. Instead we try and work it out on our own. Sometimes it works out, that's when it's God's grace on us. And then sometimes it gets worst. And that's when mercy steps in. Either way God intercedes our thoughts and actions when we call on the Lord. And it doesn't matter where you are in Christ. As a Christian, if your heart is right with the Lord, then you are not exempt from experiencing God's deliverance. Of course, we want it right away, but it is in God's time. But if there is trouble in your path, call on the Lord.

If your Spirit has been crushed, call on the Lord. And if you think your troubles are more than God can handle, just remember that God is the God over all things, even the troubles that the world may bring. So, don't fear His power, fear Him. And whatever you do, give thanks for his grace and mercy that will see you through.

Be Blessed and Always Pray!!!

Journal

YOUR ASSIGNMENT: FAITH AND TRUST

No "Juan" sharing HER(s)tory today. Just a few Words from the Word of God to encourage you to continue in the spirit with your whole heart, and not to lean to your OWN understanding, just have faith and trust the Lord, Jesus and the Holy Spirit to direct your path, bless, and deliver you in any and all circumstances and situations. Be like a tree planted by the rivers of water that sends out its roots by the stream. It does not fear when the heat comes; its leaves are always green. It has no worries in a year of drought and never fails to bear fruit (Jeremiah 17:7-8).

(Just one Juan note: I have read and pondered on Hebrews 11 many times, and every time it encourages me the more to "just stand". In all of those "faith and trust" situations and circumstances God promised to provide, and we are witnesses that He did.)

GOD'S WORD: _Hebrews 11:7-23 By faith Noah, when warned about things not yet seen, in holy fear built an ark to save his family. By his faith he condemned the world and became heir of the righteousness that is in keeping with faith. By faith Abraham, when called to go to a place he would later receive as his inheritance, obeyed, and went, even though he did not know where he was going.

By faith he made his home in the promised land like a stranger in a foreign country; he lived in tents, as did Isaac and Jacob, who were heirs with him of the same promise. For he was looking forward to the city with foundations, whose architect and builder is God.

Hebrews 11:39-40 These were all commended for their faith, yet none of them received what had been promised, since God had planned something better for us so that only together with us would they be made perfect.

Now may the Love of God be with you, the peace of Jesus maintain you and the Holy Spirit restrain you. In Jesus Name and For His Sake. Can I get an "AMEN" "AMEN" "AMEN

Journal

Hello, everyone, this is your sister Algie, praying to God for strength to get life done!

Lord, I'm listening. What is my assignment? Some days it's hard to bypass the trials that are before me. But I know there must be a lesson for each trial. There must be something for me to learn. There must be something that you are trying to teach me. I refuse to believe that we are not to learn a lesson from the things we go through. I want to share my testimonies. I want to tell the world how they can overcome.

Things will past. A New day will come. Time will move on. We will not suffer long. Alright. With this being said, let's read some encouraging words written by...

I say trials and tests locate a person. In other words, they determine where you are spiritual. They reveal the true condition of your heart. How you react to pressure is how the real you reacts. -- John Bevere

Life is 10% of what happens to you, and 90% of how you respond to it. —Unknown

There has been much tragedy in my life; at least half of it happened. -- Mark Twain

The two big advantages I had at birth were to have been born wise and to have been born in poverty. --Stevie Wonder

Bless a thing and it will bless you. Curse it and it will curse you...If you bless a situation, it has no power to hurt you, and even if it is troublesome for a time, it will gradually fade out, if you sincerely bless it. --Emmet Fox

Suffering has been stronger than all other teaching and has taught me to understand what your heart used to be. I have been bent and broken, but - I hope - into a better shape. --Charles Dickens

Blessings alone do not open our eyes. Indeed, blessings by themselves tend to close our eyes. We do not come to know Him in the blessing but in the breaking. --Chip Brogden

Most people are far more prone to let the bad experiences shape their views than the good ones. --Rick Joyner

Now some bible teachings on Faith:
James 1:6 New International Version (NIV)
But when you ask, you must believe and not doubt, because the one who doubts is like a wave of the sea, blown and tossed by the wind.
You ever say that prayer you use to say as a child: God is Great, and God is good, and we thank him for our food?

Lord today I thank you for all the food, --- wisdom strength, guidance, and Love.... I Love You Father. I ask that you Bless my friends and family. In Jesus Name and for His Sake. Amen!

Journal

From the Heart and Spirit of Sister Badia A.

Good Monday Morning to you!

Rise and Shine! God, we give you all the glory and honor for you are worthy to be praised! In Jesus name, AMEN!

You Are Mine, And I Am Yours. We Are Assigned To Each Other

Bless the Lord for hearing Adam's heart by the actions he must have had when he walked the earth for a short period alone. **Genesis 2:18-22** talks about Adams need of a helpmate which must have shown in the way he interacted with all of God's creations. Not having a helper, companion, brother, sister, or a friend must have stopped Adam's desires for tending to the land God gave him dominion over. I imagine His true assignment was not clear to him, because he lacked the one thing most of us desire to have, which is to share our assignment with another.

When we think about the assignment and our need to have a companion, (friend, husband, or wife), we think about our heart's desires. We also think about giving and sharing our most precious wants with another. It is a proven fact in my life. There are people assigned to me, and I am assigned to people. The assignment we receive to help others along the way is truly heaven sent. Think about the process of God creating Eve for Adam. God took a piece of Adam to create Eve. The fact that Eve possessed a piece of Adam, in my opinion, further explains how we possess a piece of the person God assigns us to (and vice versa).

I am encouraged by the concern God has for us. God does not just send anyone our way as a helpmate, He sends the other piece to the puzzle. The piece that helps to complete us and make us whole, eager, and able to fulfill all He created us to be. AMEN!

Encouragement/Prayer
Seek the Lord with all your heart and lean not on your own understanding. In all your ways, seek Him, and He will direct your path. With the great expectations, we must believe He can and will send us just what we need when we need it.

Proverbs 3:5-6 English Standard Version (ESV)
Trust in the LORD with all your heart,
and do not lean on your own understanding.
In all your ways acknowledge him,
and he will make straight your paths.

Father God, thank you for being the ALL in our lives. You are truly the creator of all things, and from you, all blessings flow. Thank you, Lord, for knowing everything about us. Thank you for assigning people to us. People with the purpose of fulfilling the need for relationship, and revelation. The revelation we receive is revealed through the one you send. The message is clear as the scales are wiped from our eyes, revealing your purpose for us in your Kingdom. Lord, bless us with the desire to receive the helpmate you have assigned to us. May we see the gift we hold. The gift to help grow ourselves and others in you. We love you and give you all the honor and praise. In, Jesus precious name, AMEN!

Journal

From the Heart and Spirit of Sister Monica D.

Good Morning Everyone!

Lord we thank you for this glorious day. May we find peace and comfort throughout our day and less worry and stress. In Jesus name, Amen.

Philippians 4:6-7 (NLT)
6 Don't worry about anything; instead, pray about everything. Tell God what you need and thank him for all he has done. 7 Then you will experience God's peace, which exceeds anything we can understand. His peace will guard your hearts and minds as you live in Christ Jesus.

There is peace when we learn to love like God and less like the world. There are no conditions to God's peace yet so many conditions in the world. I find my peace through prayer, spending time with God, Christian music, and quiet time with myself. Peace will allow you to find clarity in God's plan for your life. You begin to receive understanding to your purpose and assignment for your life. Peace takes the place where problems, worry, stresses of daily life use to be. We can allow peace to come in and take over the small stuff. I say small stuff because God is bigger than any problem, worry or stress that we may face.

We spend so much time trying to win the battle that only God can fight. That's why it is God who gets the glory.

God is the Prince of Peace and if we seek and ask God for peace, then He will surely comfort you and provide you the peace in everything that surpasses all of our understanding and then we can begin to hear more from God and less of the world. Remember that the battle is not ours, it is the Lord. He will fight your worries.

Prayer isn't every time I need something. Prayer is I need something every time, so I pray. Whatever the need and thank Jesus for His grace, mercy and for His power. Not necessarily for Him to give but for what He has given. Strength, love, peace, comfort.... all this matter because without them you could never see the full blessings given to you.

There is no worry where there is God, but where there is God, there is peace.

Be Blessed, and Always Pray!

Journal

No "Sister Juan" sharing HER(s)tory today. Just a song and a few words from the Lord.

Sometimes we just need a song and a word from the Lord to build our spirits, our strength and trust in God when we feel all our strength is gone. Just a thought.....

My mind goes back to a song we used to sing at Temple of Deliverance Church in Washington, DC. It went like this...Give me strength, give me strength, give me strength oh lord, oh lord. If you do, if you do oh lord, I'll tear the walls down. Joshua fought the battle around Jericho, he never fought a battle like this before, he marched around the walls seven times, then he shouted out the victory is mine, if you do, if you do oh lord I'll tear the walls down!!

The bible speaks of many instances where he gives his people strength to carry on, let me just share this one....

The Book of Joshua
Joshua is known as a great military leader. When he was a young man, he was asked to be one of the 12 spies who entered the Promised Land to see what their plan of attack should be. He was outnumbered and Moses chose to follow the crowd. The children of Israel wandered in the wilderness for 40 years. At the end of those long years, Moses turned over the leadership of Israel to Joshua.

The whole book of Joshua tells the story of how Joshua lead the people through battle after battle to inhabit the land that God had promised Abraham several hundred years before.

Joshua 6:1-5 (NIV)
Now the gates of Jericho were securely barred because of the Israelites. No one went out and no one came in. Then the LORD said to Joshua, "See, I have delivered Jericho into your hands, along with its king and its fighting men. March around the city once with all the armed men. Do this for six days. 4 Have seven priests carry trumpets of rams' horns in front of the ark. On the seventh day, march around the city seven times, with the priests blowing the trumpets. When you hear them sound a long blast on the trumpets, have the whole army give a loud shout; then the wall of the city will collapse and the army will go up, everyone straight in."

May you be encouraged by the lyrics of the song and the verses of scripture from the Word of God. I encourage you to read the book of Joshua for further insight on strength. And, if you do, I believe you will gain some insight to tear some walls down ...." just a little food for thought...

Now may the Love of God be with you, the peace of Jesus maintain you and the Holy Spirit restrain you. In Jesus

Name and For His Sake. Can I get an "AMEN" "AMEN" "AMEN

Journal

Hello, everyone, this is your Sister Algie wondering how
we get the strength to carry on with The Assignments
God gives. Life can sometimes be so sad. We're faced with
death and sickness. Yet, as Maya Angelou wrote, and

spoke so eloquently, **we Still Rise**!

After all the different trials in my life are over, I wonder HOW, just how did I do that? I realize, But God. I know it would be impossible without him.

Mathew 19:26 World English Bible
Looking at them, Jesus said, "With men this is impossible, but with God all things are possible."

I recall as a child, listening to older people, thinking their quotes, or silly sayings were weird. Now, I am the older person that has lived through some difficult times. Yet, I still smile, I have lived long enough to know that Prayer changes things, and Faith can make it seem impossible almost magical.

My wisdom lets me know that as Philippians 4:13 reads - I can do all things through Christ that strengthens me.

Do you have a closet, or a private place where you get quiet enough to hear God? To tell him all about the issues in your life. To ask him for guidance and clarity. I Pray that you are amazed, like me. Amazed at of all the Miracles that God does for us when we ask and Praise Him for His goodness and mercy. The Bible says you have not because you ask not.

Now, my Gift to you, my favorite passage in the Bible!

Mark 11:22-25 English Standard Version (ESV)

And Jesus answered them, "Have faith in God. Truly, I say to you, whoever says to this mountain, 'Be taken up and thrown into the sea,' and does not doubt in his heart, but believes that what he says will come to pass, it will be done for him. Therefore, I tell you, whatever you ask in prayer, believe that you have received it, and it will be yours. And whenever you stand praying, forgive, if you have anything against anyone, so that your Father also who is in heaven may forgive you your trespasses.

I Pray God gives you strength to achieve your life assignments. In Jesus name and for His Sake Amen

Journal

From the Heart and Spirit of Sister Badia A.

Rise and Shine! God, we give you all the glory and honor for you are worthy to be praised! In Jesus name, AMEN!

I TRUST GOD WILL DO ALL HE SAID HE WOULD DO.

HE'S ABLE!

When in tune with the acts of God, the heart is a tall, tale sign, that He can and will speak, move, reconcile, and recreate all. He will do it on your behalf, and for His purpose...

Life can throw some difficult blows our way, sometimes causing us to become overwhelmed by the arrow. We experience overwhelming feelings at times, presenting some confusing thoughts and heartfelt pain. The thoughts and feelings can blind our vision. We only see the situation we are currently standing in, causing us to sink deeper into feelings of grief and disbelief....

Well, it is time for us to trust God. Allow Him to revive the dead thoughts, replacing them with truth, hope, love, comfort, and direction. It is never our Father's intent to leave us in a dead situation. Our Savior's purpose is to free us by rebirthing a renewed way of living. In His Word, the Lord says, "I am the way and the truth and the life" (John 14:6).

We have faith and trust the Word of God. Then, He will speak, move, reconcile, and recreate our life's most difficult challenges. When our hearts are in tune with the acts of God, we gain strength. God's acts can bring great changes. Changes that will help shape us into strong believers and great achievers in our lives and for His Kingdom.

It does not matter the circumstance and/or situation. What matters most is the connection built by the reconciliation of our relationship with Christ. God can and will change ALL situations… Let me say that again, GOD CAN, and WILL CHANGE ALL situations. The only things that can stop him are us not having the faith to believe that He can and are not trusting that He will.

It is my prayer that we will allow God to do some miraculous things to and through our lives. Trust his Word and believe in the hand He extends to you. AMEN!

Journal

From the Heart and Spirit of Sister Monica D.

Good Morning Everyone!

Lord I thank You for this day. This is the day that You have made, and I am so glad to be in it. Lord, Your promises are what keep me grounded in your word. The more I read, the more I rejoice in knowing that no matter how many promises You have made, they are all Yes! In Jesus name, Amen!

2 Corinthians 1:20

For no matter, how many promises God has made, they are Yes" in Christ. And so, through him the "Amen" is spoken by us to the glory of God.

Amen! Hallelujah to You Lord knowing that all your promises to us is true and real. We don't have to think no for an answer because Your answer is yes. We say Amen to knowing that because Your word has truth, I have no room for doubt in my heart. Yes, Lord! This is what I can say on this journey to righteousness. It's because of your written word, that I know that if I fall, you will lift me up.

Yes, I will have troubles along the way, but again your word says, that a righteous man will have many troubles, but You, God, will deliver him from them all! (Psalm 34:19). And if I do wrong, I can ask for forgiveness from you and You will forgive. You have promised me that throughout my life you will never leave nor forsake me. Well Lord, I even know that if I get lost and lose my way, your word says that when my anxiety gets great within me, your consolation will bring joy to my soul. It's awesome knowing that the stronger my faith, the more promises I will experience in Christ!

Thank You, Lord for Your promises to me. I have no reason to turn back. I have no reason to think that I am alone. Thank You Lord, for I know that through faith, and because of the promise, I have purpose to get through the process to see my Victory.

Be Blessed and Always Pray!

Journal

| |
| |
| |
| |
| |
| |
| |
| |
| |
| |
| |
| |
| |

No "Juan" sharing HER(s)tory today. Just a word, and a few scriptures. Be encouraged. Continue to grow stronger in the Lord. God's strength will show up in you, wherever and whenever you need it.

Everybody is going through something, I don't know what your something is, and you don't know mine. However, I do know, and am a living witness, that if we continue to pray, trust, and believe the Lord, through Jesus Christ and the Holy Spirit, we will gain strength to make it. So today, ask the Lord to lead you to scriptures on STRENGTH. May you be strengthened with all of God's power within you, and endure with patience and joy...... Now just a little about Daniel...

Daniel in the Lion's Den—Daniel 6
Many years after the three Hebrew children were spared from the flames, there was a new king in Babylon. He and Daniel became friends. But not everyone loved Daniel as the king did. Some men tricked the king into making a law that required the people to worship him only. If they were caught worshiping any other person, idol or god, they would be thrown into a den of lions.

This law was made specifically to capture Daniel. His habit was to pray at least three times a day. The men caught Daniel praying and brought him to the king for punishment. Though King Darius was saddened at this turn of events, he still carried out the punishment he authorized.

Daniel said to the king that he would trust the Lord even if the lions killed him. The lions didn't kill Daniel though.

He was spared through the night by God. When he emerged from the lion's den the king ordered that the men who made the law be lowered down to face the same punishment they wanted for Daniel. The Bible says they did not even touch the ground before the lions consumed them.

Psalm 46: 1 God is our Refuge and Strength [mighty and impenetrable to temptation], a very present and well-proved help in trouble.

2 Corinthians 12: 9 But He said to me, My grace (My favor and loving-kindness and mercy) is enough for you [sufficient against any danger and enables you to bear the trouble manfully]; for My strength and power are made perfect (fulfilled and completed) and show themselves most effective in [your] weakness. Therefore, I will all the more gladly glory in my weaknesses and infirmities, that the strength and power of Christ (the Messiah) may rest (yes, may pitch a tent over and dwell) upon me!

Just a little food for thought....

Now may the Love of God be with you, the peace of Jesus maintain you and the Holy Spirit restrain you. In Jesus Name and For His Sake. Can I get an "AMEN" "AMEN" "AMEN".

Journal

Hello, my sisters and my brothers this again is your sister Algie encouraging you to keep the strength of God!

He makes Himself available to us. The Bible is His Word for us to read and understand.

Psalms 27: 1 "The LORD is my light and my salvation; whom shall I fear? The LORD is the strength of my life; of whom shall I be afraid?"

My Words: Whenever your mind goes through tough times, remember that God gives us clarity. This morning I was trying to figure something out and

I became overwhelmed. Standing in my shower I heard God say trust me. And my response was Thank you for reminding me again whose child I am. As soon as I walked out the bathroom, my question was answered. After I did all I could do, I gave it to God. Then, I just stood on His Word.

Just like the song says **JUST STAND** and believe that all things work together for the good to them that love God, to them who are called according to his purpose (Romans 8:28 King James Version).

A lot of strength is necessary to follow God's assignments in your life, but if you live long enough and go through some trials, there's no way you can't make it through. You learn to Trust Him. You heard that saying that Life can bring you to your knees. Well, a lot of things can and will.

The Armor of God Ephesians 10- 6-18

Finally, be strong in the Lord and in his mighty power. Put on the full armor of God, so that you can take your stand against the devil's schemes. For our struggle is not against flesh and blood, but against the rulers, against the authorities, against the powers of this dark world and against the spiritual forces of evil in the heavenly realms. Therefore, put on the full armor of God, so that when the day of evil comes, you may be able to stand your ground, and after you have done everything, to stand. Stand firm then, with the belt of truth buckled around your waist, with the breastplate of righteousness in place, and with your feet fitted with the readiness that comes from the gospel of peace. In addition to all this, take up the shield of faith, with which you can extinguish all the flaming arrows of the evil one. Take the helmet of salvation and the sword of the Spirit, which is the word of God. And pray in the Spirit on all occasions with all kinds of prayers and requests. With this in mind, be alert and always keep on praying for all the Lord's people.

I am here to tell you, get armored. I Love You. And, I always Pray for the best for you and your families.

In Jesus Name and for his Sake Amen!

Journal

From the Heart and Spirit of Sister Badia A.

Rise and Shine! God, we give you all the glory and honor for you are worthy to be praised! In Jesus name, AMEN!

RELATIONSHIP: WILL THE REAL ONES PLEASE STAND UP!

Most of us know that when it comes to relationship, generally, we seek to find a person who shares some of the same qualities as us. We find something in common, such as the movies we watch, conversations we have, and even in the clothes we wear. Our ability to relate to one another can, interestingly, be the same. Especially, if it is our desire to identify the genuine qualities in another person.

For some of us, we may have never experienced such relationships. The effects of this may cause one to shut down, withdrawn, and disconnected. Well, I'm here to share that there is a relationship that tops all relationships, all while birthing heartfelt qualities in us. Teaching us how to wholeheartedly engage with those around us. The purpose of such connections is for us to grow in heart and action. Allowing us to one day become a "relational strength" to those in need of receiving spiritual gift(s).

John 15:5-8 New International Version (NIV)

"I am the vine; you are the branches. If you remain in me and I in you, you will bear much fruit; apart from me you can do nothing. If you do not remain in me, you are like a branch that is thrown away and withers; such branches are picked up, thrown into the fire and burned. If you remain in me and my words remain in you, ask whatever you wish, and it will be done for you. This is to my Father's glory, that you bear much fruit, showing yourselves to be my disciples.

Most times, real relationship seeker's mission is to connect by sharing portions of themselves with people who may not possess the same qualities. This does not mean that the person is better than the other person. In fact, it means that they are equal.

Through love and compassion, we become passionate about linking with others. Our eagerness is an important component to the Kingdom building process. Bless the Lord for creating such relationships and affording us the ability to grown and share in Him....

Journal

From the Heart of Sister Monica D.

Good Morning Everyone!

Lord we give you thanks for this beautiful morning! We are forever grateful to You Lord for being a loving, forgiving God who provides us with all we need. We worship and adore you in Jesus name, Amen.

Scripture:

Jeremiah 29:11 (NIV) 11 For I know the plans I have for you, "declares the Lord, "plans to prosper you and not to harm you, plans to give you hope and a future.

Message:

We serve a God who not only gives us life, but he also equips us with the gifts and talents that lead us to the assignment of living for purpose. Some gifts are connected to our dreams and for some of us who believe in the dreams, understand the gifts and talents given, but for some of us, we are not sure how to follow. We become so eager to gain, we begin to lose sight, and then lose hope in making the dreams reality Not only do we fail to realize our needs, God also lets us know that even though we fail, attempt to give up, even sin against our own nature in order to get it our way, God favors us through it all.

For the gifts and calling of God, gifts which God has bestowed upon us, with which he has favored us, he will

never revoke. Follow your dream and never give up. God doesn't change His mind, we do. That's the glory of His perfection! Therefore, we are to receive what's for us! Hallelujah, Glory be to God for He is Awesome!

Be Blessed and Always Pray!!!

Journal

No "Juan" sharing HER(s)tory today. Just a word, STRONGER, lyrics from a song, a portion of scripture. Be encouraged. Continue to grow stronger in the Lord. God's strength will show up in you, wherever and whenever you need it.

LYRICS: Never Would Have Made It by Marvin Sapp (You may listen to it on YouTube at www.youtube.com/watch?v=7JXFg5KEoXg.)

Never would have made it. Never could have made it, without you. I would have lost it all. But now I see how you were there for me. And I can say. Never would have made it. Never could have made it without you. I would have lost it all but now I see how you were there for me and I can say. I'm stronger, I'm wiser I'm better, much better. When I look back over all you brought me through I can see that you were the one I held on to. And. I never, never would have made it...

SCRIPTURE: Samson—Judges 13-16

The physical strength of Samson was given by God. Because of promises that Samson's parents had made to the Lord, Samson was a powerful man whom God used to fight Israel's enemy. Though God worked through him, Samson did not always obey the Lord. Samson accomplished much in his own physical strength, but it wasn't until he trusted in what God could do through him that he was able to accomplish his greatest victory.

Samson was a Nazarite from birth. A Nazarite is someone who makes certain sacrifices to serve the Lord in a special way. Most of the time the vow of a Nazarite is taken for a limited period and for a specific purpose. However, Samson was dedicated to the Lord before he was born. He was to be a Nazarite for life. Part of his vow was that his hair would never be shaved from his head. In return, God gave him an unbelievable strength.

As Samson grew, he did not obey his parents nor the Lord. God still used him to fight the enemy. Sadly, he was doing it in his own physical strength instead of trusting God to guide him. His strength was given by God because of his vow as a Nazarite. But Samson grew to believe that he did not need God or his vow to have the physical strength that he enjoyed in life. Samson told Delilah (a Philistine woman and an enemy) that he would lose his strength if his hair was shaved. The result was that Samson was captured by the enemy and was made a slave. His eyes were gouged out and the enemy made a mockery of him and the God of Israel. Samson learned that his strength did come from God. He asked God to allow him to perform one final act of strength. This time he trusted in God and was able to kill more of the enemy in his final work for God than he did his whole life.

Just a little food for thought....

Now may the Love of God be with you, the peace of Jesus maintain you and the Holy Spirit restrain you. In Jesus Name and For His Sake. Can I get an "AMEN" "AMEN" "AMEN

Journal

Hello, everyone, this is your sister Algie praying to God that I fulfill my God Given Assignment to encourage you in His word!

The Scene - Thursday night after work. I did not feel good at work, the devil was trying to steal my Peace! What should I do. Go home, but will I be comfortable enough to just relax. My neck is hurting, and I do not know why. So, I decided to go to the hospital. I chose the place that people generally speak about negatively. However, I went anyway. It was on my way home.

As I sit in the waiting room, I'm impatient. I do not feel special. Did they not hear what I said? I don't feel well. Why have I been here 2 hours, just waiting.

First, I'm sitting on the wrong side of the waiting room. When I asked a lady if I was sitting on the right side, she seemed a little irritated. Another person

waiting had children that were running up and down the hallways, running and screaming. Alright I'm not feeling too Peaceful right now.

Suddenly, I heard a voice say start writing your devotional now! I thought how? My Phone is about to die.

I don't have paper. However, when God speaks, nothing can stop His commands. His Assignments over your life. I found a pen and two envelopes. At first the pen did not write. BUT GOD! He makes everything possible. Ink started flowing. My whole attitude began to change. All the circumstances seemed different.

Thankful is how I'm feeling now. The pain that I was feeling is starting to subside. The kids are playing like kids do. I'm waiting because I'm not that bad off. I am receiving Peace because I am expecting Peace. I tell you this, I don't even want to stop writing because I want to stay in His Spirit.

Thank You for Peace. Thank You for comforting me. I Thank You Father for taking my mind off myself. I Love YOU GOD.

Less than 3 minutes after I finished writing, the nurse called me to the back. I accept my calling to encourage. FIND YOUR PEACE. IT IS THERE ALL THE TIME!
Amen

Journal

From the Heart and Spirit of Sister Badia A.

Good Monday Morning to you!

Rise and Shine! God, we give you all the glory and honor for you are worthy to be praised! In Jesus name, AMEN!

DREAM KILLERS....

If we let them, Dream Killers will snatch the life God has for us. They will snatch our life through persuasion, manipulation, temptation, and deceit. Protect the dreams. Allow yourself to visually view you as worthy and capable to fulfill your assignment.
How many of us know that there are specific people assigned to help birth the dreams or visions God purposed for you? The presence of the dreams and visions is just as important as you are to achieve the call. They too have been called to fill a great purpose in the Kingdom. However, to bring it all to fruition, it takes connecting with likeminded people....

Now, on the other hand... There are people in our lives who do not understand that they too have purposed assignments created by God, so they look at you and "your dream" or "vision" as a threat. The ill thoughts they carry are not necessarily against you, but they are meant to destroy the very thing God created in you....

This is trick of the enemy 101. His first priority (so he thinks) is to seek and destroy the relationships we have with one another. It starts with the way we accept and receive each other's Godly abilities. The bigger picture is snuffed out by the thought(s) and or questions, which most times are "Who do they think they are?" or "Why not me?"

It is sad how we allow the enemy to manipulate our inner man. We must take the time to listen and hear what the other person has to say. But, then again, it is not for us to always share our dreams or visions with everyone.

God assigns people to hear and encourage us during our digesting stage of understanding our assignment. There are certain people sent our way to assist us and help us to grow. And, most importantly, there are people who are sent by God to help birth and carry out the assignment. Together, we can do some great and awesome things for the Kingdom.

We know this to be true, because we see it when we read the story of Joseph (Genesis 37). We learn that dream killers come in different forms. Most times they can be a family member, friend, and/or a new acquaintance. A dream killer's mission is to destroy the dream. The purpose we have as dreamers and visionaries is to accept, grow, protect, and fulfill our assignment (s).

Ending Question?
Which are you? Are you the dreamer/visionary or the dream killer? What has God given you regarding your

assignment? It is time for us to stand strong in our position and not become puffed up by the assignment. We should gain strength through the wisdom and knowledge given to us by the Holy Spirit. And, we must discern how to protect and fulfill it. and not become puffed up by the assignment.

Journal

From the Heart and Spirit of Sister Monica D.

Good Morning Everyone!

Lord thank you for Peace! I know Lord that if I keep my eyes, heart, and mind on You, I know that I am guarded and protected by your word which is my armor. With peace, I know that You have again given me comfort to know that it is done. In Jesus' name, Amen!

Do you ever wonder what people see when they look at you? Some days I can be so withdrawn in thoughts, I go into thinking, I wonder how others see me today? I know that at some point in my day, I will have said an encouraging word to someone or give my best to whatever they may need, and it always remind me why I do what I do. And who it is I do it for. It is always for God. What I have come to realize that when most people see me as calm, and without worry, and able to encourage them, when I sometimes need the encouraging myself, they only see the peace where God has taken my troubles away, and replaced it with his love, joy and peace.

The glow that God's presence is in your life shows a sense of peace where there should be pain, peace where there should be sorrow and peace where there should be shame. You see the God that I serve is God who His word says in Philippians 4:4-7 (NKJV)4 Rejoice in the Lord

always. Again, I will say, rejoice! 5 Let your gentleness be known to all men. The Lord is at hand. 6 Be anxious for nothing, but in everything by prayer and supplication, with thanksgiving, let your requests be made known to God; 7 and the peace of God, which surpasses all understanding, will guard your hearts and minds through Christ Jesus. I always rejoice in the Lord , for the good and the bad times. So when I give it all over to God, its shows through the peace that glows through my spirit that makes you wonder where is my worry, where is my pain, where is the sorrow and where is the shame? You must know that we serve a God that will take all your troubles over and protect you from all the strife. And trade it all for peace, joy, and love. You wouldn't believe it! And People will see it! It shows through your everyday walk in Christ. So, when you see the joy and happiness on my face, know it isn't me, it's the peace through God's grace.

Journal

YOUR ASSIGNMENT: TRIALS TO TRAIN US

From the heart and spirit of Sister Juan sharing biblical scriptures and HER(s)tory without wavering. 2 Timothy 3:16-17 (NIV) "All scripture is God-breathed and is useful for teaching, rebuking, correcting and training in righteousness, so that the man of God may be thoroughly equipped for every good work."

I recently read somewhere that "when we let our trials train us in holiness, we will reap the peaceful fruit of righteousness and compliance with the will of our Lord bringing joy to His Heart".

With that said, I was pondering (for a couple of days) on what to share with you regarding trials that train us. On yesterday, my mind ran back to my early Christian life and an incident that contributed to my growth and dependence on the Lord, Jesus, and the Holy Spirit to lead, guide, instruct and grow me to continue towards completing my assignment(s) here on earth. Want to hear it, well here it is ...one of many of my assignments and lessons learned to date.

During my early days after I accepted Christ as my Savior, I was going through some struggles at home because I had changed, and my husband had not. One evening, after returning from a stressful day at work, I came home, the house was a mess, and ketchup was running down the front of the freezer. I lost it, I screamed, asked God, why I had to go through this, that I was the "saved one" and I should not be working hard, and coming home to mess, and someone who appears not to care, you know the "why me scenario". I decided to leave everything as it was and go to prayer service.

Glory to God this turned out to be my night of deliverance and the complete indwelling of the Holy Spirit. That night during the alter prayer, the Holy Spirit gripped me, whispering directions and deliverance in my ears; I don't remember all the things He revealed to me as well as others in the service. I do remember that the Spirit spoke in ways I never experienced before, revealing things that I did not have a full understanding of at that time. Told me that patience was a virtue; to take off my shoes, that the ground I was standing on was holy ground; bonded me and a Jewish friend as sisters in Christ, changed my demeanor, and started to prepare me for things I never imaged would transpire in my life.

That happened at Temple of Deliverance Church around 1973. The Reverend Debbie Tate prophesied at the end of the service, how the Spirit had taken us into a different rim and of all the deliverances and other spiritual things that were in store for us. The service lasted almost four hours. I was so happy and overjoyed,

just could not stop smiling. In the midst of such joy, I began to think how I had dropped my husband at my sister-in-law's while I attended prayer service, and I thought he was going to be so upset that I took so long to return to pick him up. When I arrived at my sister-in-law's, he had been drinking and did not even realized how long I had been gone (divine intervention). Like I said, some of God's revelations on that night I cannot remember, but I will never forget that night!

Since that night, I have experienced many situations and circumstances (shared a few with you) that have brought instructions, deliverance, Holy Spirit sharing moments, passing grades, and a growth in Christ that is beyond what I expected that night. May I repeat again, I will never forget that night!!!

Hebrews 12:11 (NIV) says "For the moment all discipline seems painful rather than pleasant, but later it yields the peaceful fruit of righteousness to those who have been trained by it."

Ephesians 4:11-16 (NIV) says "So Christ himself gave the apostles, the prophets, the evangelists, the pastors and teachers, to equip his people for works of service, so that the body of Christ may be built up until we all reach unity in the faith and in the knowledge of the Son of God and become mature, attaining to the whole measure of the fullness of Christ. Then we will no longer be infants, tossed back and forth by the waves, and blown here and

there by every wind of teaching and by the cunning and craftiness of people in their deceitful scheming. Instead, speaking the truth in love, we will grow to become in every respect the mature body of him who is the head, that is, Christ. From him the whole body, joined and held together by every supporting ligament, grows and builds itself up in love, as each part does its work."

Now may the Love of God be with you, the peace of Jesus maintain you and the Holy Spirit restrain you. In Jesus Name and For His Sake. Can I get an "AMEN" "AMEN" "AMEN

Journal

| |
| |
| |
| |
| |
| |
| |
| |
| |
| |
| |
| |

Hello, everyone, this is your sister Algie Praying to God that I fulfill my God Given Assignment to encourage you in His word!

Peace? As I sit in my house there are children all around me. The sounds are loud with laughter that sounds like it's coming from the pits of their stomachs.

That must be a Peace that I forgot. I'm going to try to think like a child once a day. I want to look back at all my challenges and wonder how I got over.

Philippians 4:7 King James Version (KJV) And the peace of God, which Passeth all understanding, shall keep your hearts and minds through Christ Jesus.

Isaiah 26:3."Thou wilt keeps him in perfect peace whose mind is stayed on thee;"

Carrie Steckl wrote a blog on how to achieve peace in 20 ways.

Here are 10:
1. Make a personal commitment to nonviolence.
2. When you see someone in trouble, whether he or she is lost, confused, upset, or has fallen, don't act like you don't see the person – provide some help.
3. Show a child how to achieve calmness through deep breathing.
4. Show a child how to be kind to animals.

5. Show a child how to be kind to vulnerable people – the homeless, those with physical or cognitive disabilities, older people, and anyone else that appears different to

the child.

6. Speak out against prejudice and discrimination when you see it.

7. When you feel angry, count to ten before saying anything. Then, ask yourself what response will be best for the greater good.

8. When you feel slighted, ask yourself if what happened was really about you or if it was about the other person.

9. When you realize that it was about the other person, find in your heart some compassion for that person, realizing that he or she is most surely struggling.

10. Regard people who hurt your feelings as your personal teachers of how to maintain a peaceful nature.

I say smile and put peace in your heart on purpose. Make Peace an action that when people encounter you, they will not forget you. I love you! And always want the best for you. In Jesus Name and for His sake Amen!

Journal

From the Heart of Sister Badia A.

Good Monday Morning to you!

Rise and Shine! God, we give you all the glory and honor for you are worthy to be praised! In Jesus name, AMEN!

RELATIONSHIP: WILL THE REAL ONES PLEASE STAND UP!

Most of us know that when it comes to relationship, generally, we seek to find a person who shares some of the same qualities as us. We find something in common, such as the movies we watch, conversations we have, and even in the clothes we wear. Our ability to relate to one another can, interestingly, be the same. Especially, if it is our desire to identify the genuine qualities in another person.

For some of us, we may have never experienced such relationships. The effects of this may cause one to shut down, withdrawn, and disconnected. Well, I am here to share that there is a relationship that tops all relationships, all while birthing heartfelt qualities in us. Teaching us how to wholeheartedly engage with those around us. The purpose of such connections is for us to grow in heart and action. Allowing us to one day become a "relational strength" to those in need of receiving spiritual gift(s).

John 15:5-8 New International Version (NIV)

"I am the vine; you are the branches. If you remain in me and I in you, you will bear much fruit; apart from me you can do nothing. If you do not remain in me, you are like a branch that is thrown away and withers; such branches are picked up, thrown into the fire and burned. If you remain in me and my words remain in you, ask whatever you wish, and it will be done for you. This is to my Father's glory, that you bear much fruit, showing yourselves to be my disciples.

Most times, real relationship seeker's mission is to connect by sharing portions of themselves with people who may not possess the same qualities. This does not mean that the person is better than the other person. In fact, it means that they are equal.

Through love and compassion, we become passionate about linking with others. Our eagerness is an important component to the Kingdom building process. Bless the Lord for creating such relationships and affording us the ability to grown and share in Him....

Journal

From the Heart and Spirit of Monica D.

Good Morning Everyone!

Lord we thank you for this glorious day. May we find peace and comfort throughout our day and less worry and stress. In Jesus name, Amen

Philippians 4:6-7 (NLT)

Don't worry about anything; instead, pray about everything. Tell God what you need and thank him for all he has done. Then you will experience God's peace, which exceeds anything we can understand. His peace will guard your hearts and minds as you live in Christ Jesus.

There is a peace when we learn to love like God and less like the world. There are no conditions to God's peace yet so many conditions in the world. I find my peace through prayer, spending time with God, Christian music and quiet time with myself. Peace will allow you to find clarity in God's plan for your life. You begin to receive understanding to your purpose and assignment for your life. Peace takes the place where problems, worry, stresses of daily life use to be. We can allow peace to come in and take over the small stuff. I say small stuff because God is bigger than any problem, worry or stress that we may face.

We spend so much time trying to win the battle that only God can fight. That's why it is God who gets the glory.

God is the Prince of Peace and if we seek and ask God for peace, then He will surely comfort you and provide you the peace in everything that surpasses all of our understanding and then we can begin to hear more from God and less of the world. Remember that the battle is not ours, it is the Lord's. He will fight your worries.

Prayer is not every time I need something. Prayer is I need something every time, so I pray. Whatever the need and thank Jesus for His grace, mercy and for his power. Not necessarily for Him to give but for what He has given. Strength, love peace comfort.... All these matters because without them you could never see the full blessings given to you.

There is no worry where is God, but where there is God, there is peace.

Journal

YOUR ASSIGNMENT: GIVE ME STRENGTH

No "Juan" sharing HER(s)tory today. Just a few words from the Word of God to encourage your STRENGTH. How many times have we said "I just don't have the strength". Then, you start praying, asking the Lord to give you strength to endure, and he leads you to the portions of scripture that say… I am your strength, trust Me (Psalm 28:7-8), or wait on Me, take heart and be strong in Me (Psalm 27:14). The joy of the Lord is your strength. I read or heard this biblical story about God given strength. Want to hear it, here it is …

Shadrach, Meshach and Abednego

King Nebuchadnezzar built an idol to show his own power and strength in the world. He commanded all of the inhabitants of Babylon to bow and worship his creation. There was to be a great ceremony in which the people would worship together. When the ceremony began everyone bowed to the idol except three young Hebrew men—Shadrach, Meshach and Abednego. The three men had been brought from Israel as slaves, yet through time they were promoted to positions of authority because of their great wisdom. When it was time to worship the image, they stood strong because of their belief in the God of Israel.

For not obeying the king's command, they were sentenced to be burned in a furnace. The king was so angry at their disobedience that he demanded the furnace be heated seven times more than normal for the trio. The

Bible says that the furnace was so hot that the soldiers who threw the three men in were consumed by the fire.

Shadrach, Meshach and Abednego were not harmed in any way. The ropes which bound them were burned away, but they walked about freely in the fire. Nebuchadnezzar said that he saw them walking around with a fourth person who he believed was the Son of God. For their strength and trust in God, the king proclaimed his trust in the God of Israel.

I encourage you to read Daniel 3 for insight on strength, and how Shadrach, Meshach and Abednego's strength in the Lord lead King Nebuchadnezzar to proclaim "praise to the God of who has sent his angel and rescued his servants. They trusted in him...." just a little food for thought...

Now may the Love of God be with you, the peace of Jesus maintain you and the Holy Spirit restrain you. In Jesus Name and For His Sake. Can I get an "AMEN" "AMEN" "AMEN

Journal

HELLO EVERYONE, this is YOUR Sister Algie as always Praying to God for Encouragement for you and me!

Today I ask God for Mercy, Guidance and for His wisdom. Lord I ask You for the know how in completing the tasks of this world. Today I woke up with remnants of yesterday still in my mind.

I Had. . .Breast Cancer 9 yrs. ago, had my mammogram yesterday, all clear. Also had GYN appointment; tests done praying all is clear. But I know whatever the results, God will never leave nor forsake me.

If that is true for me, I know it's also true for you.

I tell you, after leaving both offices, my mind was all over the place. I am Praying on the table in the dressing room, on the way home, I am trying to avoid the what ifs. My body is sore, I feel like a child. I need my mommy.

I am almost 62, momma is with the Lord. I will be alright; I am thankful to have a platform to share how I feel. And to let you know that things happen. But God! We will make it through.

Thank You God for my eyes to see and ears to hear.
Having Faith ....Romans 8:28 (NIV)
And we know that in all things God works for the good of those who love him, who have been called according to his purpose.

It is a beautiful day. The sun is shining, the grass is green, and we are here.

Thank you for another opportunity.

Revelation 21:4 (NIV) "He will wipe every tear from their eyes. There will be no more death or mourning or crying or pain, for the old order of things has passed away."

In Jesus Name and for His Sake Amen.

Journal

From the Heart and Spirit of Sister Badia A.

Good Monday Morning to you!

Rise and Shine! God, we give you all the glory and honor for you are worthy to be praised! In Jesus name, AMEN!

RELATIONSHIPS. IT IS UP TO YOU TO DISCERN THEIR PURPOSE IN YOUR LIFE...

We want to believe that the people we meet are meant to be active and present in our lives. In some cases, the relationship(s) we pursue can turn out to be a hindrance to our assignment, and not active components of self and spiritual growth.

Just think about the connections you have made over the years. Think about the role each one has contributed to your spiritual journey. Have they intrigued you to look deeper into who you are in the relationship, or have you learned just how volatile he or she may be in helping you reach the goal?

Let us look at the relationship Jesus had with His twelve disciples. Each one had an important role, to follow Christ, spread His Word, and to continue to grow the church after His death. I imagine Jesus' ability to discern who would be the right men to join him on His journey. Flaws and all Jesus chose them based upon their trust and the heart they had to follow Him.

Luke 6:12-13 New International Version (NIV)

One of those days Jesus went out to a mountainside to pray and spent the night praying to God. When morning came, he called his disciples to him and chose twelve of them, whom he also designated apostles:

When it comes to the connections we make in life, we must be mindful of the intentions of the other person. How to become mindful, you ask? Take some time out and pray, asking the Holy Spirit to help you discern the person's purpose in your assignment. There are good and bad relationships. Both come with a purpose. One is sent to help nurture and encourage. The other is sent to tear down and destroy you. We know this is so, as we reflect on Judas' role in turning Jesus over to the chief priests who wanted to kill him (Luke 22).

Encouragement

I pray and encourage you to be mindful of the relationships you keep. It does not matter if they are meant for good or bad. What matters most is how you react to them. Will you open your heart to the help God sends to you, or will you gain strength from those who are sent to destroy and kill your assignment? Take some time and let that sink in.......

Journal

From the Heart and Spirit of Sister Monica D.

Good Day Everyone!!!!

Blessed is the one who serves the Lord. Blessed is the one who's eye, heart and mind is on God! In Jesus name, Amen!

Proverbs 29:18 (NIV) Where there is no revelation, people cast off restraint; but blessed is the one who heeds wisdom's instruction.

When people do not accept divine guidance, they run wild. But whoever obeys the law is joyful.

When we refuse to accept God's will in our lives, we can lose control, and this can cause us to sin and be stuck in sin. But when you see it and accept it, you will live a life of obedience by teaching others and serving God's will of bringing souls closer to Christ.

Revelation 1:3 (NIV) Blessed is the one who reads aloud the words of this prophecy and blessed are those who hear it and take to heart what is written in it because the time is near.

Do not live a life of blindness and unrevealed love when once you accept Christ, there is a life worth living. Be blessed as it is revealed in God's Holy word. Receive God, repent of your sins and allow God to reveal to You His power.

Journal

No "Sister Juan" sharing HER(s)tory today, just sharing a biblical publication posted by Margaret Lepke for you to research and ponder on.

Relationship Advice from God

What better way to learn about happy relationships within God's family than getting advice straight from God's Word? If you follow His instructions, your relationships will begin to blossom...

"This is God's commandment: that we should believe on the name of His Son Jesus Christ and love one another, as He gave us commandment."
(1 John 3:23)

❤ Love one another (John 13:35) - This command appears 16 times!

❤ Devote yourself to one another (Romans 12:10)

❤ Honour others above yourselves (Romans 12:10)

❤ Live in harmony with one another (Romans 12:16)

❤ Build up one another (Romans 14:19; 1 Thessalonians 5:11)

❤ Be like-minded towards one another (Romans 15:5)

❤ Accept one another (Romans 15:7)

❤ Admonish one another (Romans 15:14; Colossians 3:16)

❤ Care for one another (1 Corinthians 12:25)

💜 Serve one another (Galatians 5:13)

💜 Carry one another's burdens (Galatians 6:2)

💜 Forgive one another (Ephesians 4:2, 32; Colossians 3:13)

💜 Be patient with one another (Ephesians 4:2; Colossians 3:13)

💜 Be kind and compassionate to one another (Ephesians 4:32)

💜 Speak to one another with psalms, hymns and spiritual songs

(Ephesians 5:19)

💜 Submit to one another (Ephesians 5:21, 1 Peter 5:5)

💜 Consider others better than yourselves (Philippians 2:3)

💜 Look to the interests of others, not just your own (Philippians 2:4)

💜 Bear with one another (Colossians 3:13)

💜 Teach one another (Colossians 3:16)

💜 Comfort one another (1 Thessalonians 4:18)

💜 Encourage one another (Hebrews 3:13)

💜 Stir up one another to love and good works (Hebrews 10:24)

💜 Be hospitable to one another (1 Peter 4:9)

💜 Use the gifts that God has given us for the benefit of one another

(1 Peter 4:10)

💜 Clothe yourselves with humility towards one another (1 Peter 5:5)

💜 Pray for one another (James 5:16)

♥ Confess our faults to one another (James 5:16)

♥ Rejoice with those who rejoice; morn with those who mourn (Rom.12:15)

"Therefore, whatever you do, do all to the glory of God!" (1 Corinthians 10:31)

Now may the Love of God be with you, the peace of Jesus maintain you and the Holy Spirit restrain you. In Jesus Name and For His Sake. Can I get an "AMEN" "AMEN" "AMEN

Journal

Hello Everybody. This is your Sister Algie, praying to God for wisdom and strength. Just want to let you know how much He loves you. He wants the best for us even when we don't recognize it.

1 John 4:16 ESV So we have come to know and to believe the love that God has for us. God is love, and whoever abides in love abides in God, and God abides in Him.

Relationships

God is eternal. This is the best relationship we will ever have. How can that be? We can't touch Him, but we can feel Him. We can't see Him, but we know He's there. He's just awesome!

My relationship with God, is one that if I worry, it's not for long. Time and experience has shown me the amazing things God can do. Year after year, it is almost unexplainable, the miraculous things He has done in my life. With God nothing is impossible. He gives us the opportunity to share His goodness with one another. He gave us the Bible as a spiritual guide, to help us along our journey.

God's Word has the answers to some of the most important questions about life decisions and the direction for us to achieve our goals. Pick it up. Read it. You can even download the bible app on your phone. Doing so will help you understand the importance of connecting with Christ.

God Bless you. And, remember that the most important relationship you will ever have is with your Father God! Amen, and Amen.

Journal

From the Heart and Spirit of Sister Badia A.

Good Monday Morning to you!

Rise and Shine! God, we give you all the glory and honor for you are worthy to be praised! In Jesus name, AMEN!

WHEN THE SAINTS COME MARCHING IN

When the Saints come marching in, O when the Saints come marching in, Lord, I want to be in the number, when the Saints come marching in. The adult choir would sing this song while marching down the aisle of the church. I remember looking at the stride in their walk and the swaying of their arms. I thought wow, I want to be in the number. I want to march in that line singing for the Lord.

Wow! It was not until I was older that I found out that there is a real army of people living for God. This army of people are multiple in number, more than anyone could count. They are cleansed and transformed into soldiers of the cross. I still feel excited about the power of God and His ability to cleanse us of ALL sin, illness and shame. His power is awesome and great. I daily strive to continue in that number. It brings me great passion to sing of His greatness. AMEN!

In the Book of Revelations, we learn about the "Great Multitudes in White Robes." We learn that they are cleansed and protected by the power of God. Revelation Chapter 7: 9-10 New International Version reads "9 after this I looked, and there before me was a great multitude that no one could count, from every nation, tribe, people and language, standing before the throne and before the Lamb. They were wearing white robes and were holding palm branches in their hands. 10 And they cried out in a loud voice: "Salvation belongs to our God, who sits on the throne, and to the Lamb."

As I read this portion of scripture, I began to praise the Lord for being God the creator of ALL things. Our Lord does not discriminate or push his children aside for not being the same. Our ethnicity, shades of color, nor language defines our position in line. Our Belief in Him and a trusting heart determines our place at His throne. At His throne, we ALL are welcome to worship Him. We all are welcome to fellowship with one another as we join with ALL of heaven in the corporate praise of different languages. Hallelujah! What great Revelation it is to know that one day we will ALL be able to commune together in our heavenly home. AMEN!

Encouragement:

How can I become one of the multitudes in white robes? Accept the Lord Jesus Christ as Lord and Savior and believe that He rose on the third day. Allow Him to deliver you, setting you free from the life you lived in sin. Now walk in His love, peace and grace. Share the good news of Jesus Christ to all who have ears to hear. I will be praying with you. I hope you will pray for me.... See you at the throne!

Journal

From the Heart and Spirit of Sister Monica D.

Good Day Everyone!!!!

Blessed is the one who serves the Lord. Blessed is the one who's eye, heart and mind is on God! In Jesus name, Amen!

Proverbs 29:18 (NIV) Where there is no revelation, people cast off restraint; but blessed is the one who heeds wisdom's instruction.

When people do not accept divine guidance, they run wild. But whoever obeys the law is joyful.

When we refuse to accept God's will in our lives, we can lose control, and this can cause us to sin and be stuck in sin. But when you see it and accept it, you will live a life of obedience by teaching others and serving God's will of bringing souls closer to Christ.

Revelation 1:3 (NIV) Blessed is the one who reads aloud the words of this prophecy and blessed are those who hear it and take to heart what is written in it because the time is near.

Do not live a life of blindness and unrevealed love when once you accept Christ, there is a life worth living. Be blessed as it is revealed in God's Holy word. Receive God, repent of your sins and allow God to reveal to You His power.

Journal

| |
| |
| |
| |
| |
| |
| |
| |
| |
| |
| |
| |

YOUR ASSIGNMENT: GOD'S RELATIONSHIP WITH ME, MY RELATIONSHIP WITH HIM

No "Sister Juan" sharing HER(s)tory today, just a couple verses of scripture for you to ponder.

Psalm 42:2 (NIV)
My soul thirsts for God, for the living God. When can I go and meet with God?

Romans 12:1-21 (NIV)
A Living Sacrifice-- Therefore, I urge you, brothers and sisters, in view of God's mercy, to offer your bodies as a living sacrifice, holy and pleasing to God—this is your true and proper worship. Do not conform to the pattern of this world but be transformed by the renewing of your mind. Then you will be able to test and approve what God's will is—his good, pleasing and perfect will. Humble Service in the Body of Christ -- For by the grace given me I say to every one of you: Do not think of yourself more highly than you ought, but rather think of yourself with sober judgment, in accordance with the faith God has distributed to each of you. For just as each of us has one body with many members, and these members do not all have the same function, so in Christ we, though many, form one body, and each member belongs to all the others. We have different gifts,

according to the grace given to each of us. If your gift is prophesying, then prophesy in accordance with your faith; if it is serving, then serve; if it is teaching, then teach; if it is to encourage, then give encouragement; if it is giving, then give generously; if it is to lead, do it diligently; if it is to show mercy, do it cheerfully.

Love in Action -- Love must be sincere. Hate what is evil; cling to what is good. Be devoted to one another in love. Honor one another above yourselves. Never be lacking in zeal, but keep your spiritual fervor, serving the Lord. Be joyful in hope, patient in affliction, faithful in prayer. Share with the Lord's people who are in need. Practice hospitality. Bless those who persecute you; bless and do not curse. Rejoice with those who rejoice; mourn with those who mourn. Live in harmony with one another. Do not be proud, but be willing to associate with people of low position. Do not be conceited. Do not repay anyone evil for evil. Be careful to do what is right in the eyes of everyone. If it is possible, as far as it depends on you, live at peace with everyone. Do not take revenge, my dear friends, but leave room for God's wrath, for it is written: "It is mine to avenge; I will repay," says the Lord. On the contrary: "If your enemy is hungry, feed him; if he is thirsty, give him something to drink. In doing this, you will heap burning coals on his head." Do not be overcome by evil but overcome evil with good.

Now may the Love of God be with you, the peace of Jesus maintain you and the Holy Spirit restrain you. In Jesus Name and For His Sake. Can I get an "AMEN" "AMEN" "AMEN

Journal

Hello again Everybody. This is your Sister Algie, encouraging, through God, the most important Relationship You or I can ever have.

I believe that our relationship with God is the start of any successful union between our parents, friends or family. God is Love right? So, if that's true then we can never love anything or anyone without God being in our hearts. I am so thankful for this knowledge.

There are a lot of ways we can say our relationship with God started. Some find Him in their tribulation. I find Him in the sunrise, in the sky, in a baby's face. And, yes definitely when I am having a hard time.

One night I was worrying about my troubles, my health and God showed up. My house was full of people but in my mind I felt alone. My body was ailing and I needed the most important Person I know, and that was Jesus!

Isn't that something. We can cry and laugh at the same time. I love God. For my life, I would not change it. I'll never deny Him.

Merriam Webster defines relationship as.....
1: the state of being related or interrelated
• studied the relationship between the variables
2: the relation connecting or binding participants in a relationship: such as Kinship.

What is a biblical relationship?
There are different areas of relationships (dating, marriage, church, friendship, etc.), but for a biblical relationship, it must be in accordance with the teachings

of Scripture. The word, "biblical" is an adjective and simply describes the relationship as one that meets the criterion of the Bible as it defines, describes, and delineates the principles that should characterize any relationship.

Keep God first in your life, make Him the most important. You will always have Him to lean on no matter what you go through. In Jesus Name and for His Sake Amen!

Journal

From the Heart and Spirit of Sister Badia A.

Good Monday Morning to you!

Rise and Shine! God, we give you all the glory and honor for you are worthy to be praised! In Jesus name, AMEN!

Life can be difficult when our mind does not comprehend the wisdom given to us when we meditate on the Word of God. During this time of confusion, our mind goes through a series of misunderstandings. Misunderstandings from the misfortunes that life throws our way. The body loses its strength because of the mental mistakes we have endured. However, these types of dysfunctions are only temporary, because of the relationship we have with God.

1 Timothy 6:12 English Standard Version (ESV)
Fight the good fight of the faith. Take hold of the eternal life to which you were called and about which you made the good confession in the presence of many witnesses.

Our father gives us the ability to fight our battles. He produces spiritual strength in us, so we grow stronger in Him. As God's children, we are called to commune with Him. Then, we receive all that is needed to maintain our trust and faith in Him. We openly confess to all who have the ear to hear the good news that Jesus is Lord. We tell all about the miraculous blessings He gives us. The more we speak of His great grace, the more strength we receive to journey deeper in Him.

To fight the good fight does not mean it will be easy. However, it does mean that we can fight it with a clear mind, focusing on who God is. He is our provider and friend.

Psalm 46:1-3 English Standard Version (ESV)
God is our refuge and strength, a very present help in
trouble. Therefore, we will not fear though the earth gives
way, though the mountains be moved into the heart of
the sea, though its waters roar and foam, though the
mountains tremble at its swelling. Selah

Bless the Lord for the provision(s) to stand strong, and
withstand our mental, physical, and most importantly
our spiritual composure. During life's most trying and
difficult trials, it is through His blood that we are covered
and protected from the enemy.

Encouragement
Speak life to your situations. Because of the new life,
given to us by our Lord, we have the mindset to fight and
overcome ALL that may come our way. We lean on our
provider for His mercy and grace. We boldly walk in our
circumstances. Have faith and trust your assignment.
Receive the strength to do so. And, most importantly,
bless the Lord for affording you the tools to fight the good
fight. Always proclaim who He is to you, and what He is
in your life. AMEN

Journal

From the Heart and Spirit of Sister Monica D.

Good Morning Everyone!!!

Lord we thank You for lifting us up and carrying us on our way. May we give peace, love, and joy throughout our day to those who need You, In Jesus name, Amen!!!

Scripture:

Acts 20:35 (NKJV)

35 I have shown you in every way, by laboring like this, that you must support the weak. And remember the words of the Lord Jesus, that He said, 'It is more blessed to give than to receive.'"

Message:

Peace can be given to others in the way that you treat them. A smile, saying hello, or just a quick wave of your hand to acknowledge someone's presence can change a person's day. We never know what challenges a person is facing, and we know that some of life's challenges can be a heavy load. But when we go out of our way to greet, encourage or to just smile at someone, it can change their perspective on the outcome of that challenge, the outcome of their day, or for that moment.

Be pleasing to God and share the gospel with joy in your hearts. willing to give up time, love, peace and encouragement, asking God to guide us towards those who are seeking Him. Be pleasing to God and share the gospel with joy in your hearts. willing to give up time, love, peace and encouragement, asking God to guide us towards those who are seeking Him.

We may not be able to give physically but spiritually we can fulfill one's need through faith. And when you have a willing heart to do so, God will bless those who are obedient and are willing to give for another to receive. Let the Christ in you shine its light today, give some of your peace to those that seek it.

Journal

VERSIONS OF GOD'S WORD!!!

From the heart and spirit of Sister Juan sharing biblical scriptures and HER(s)tory without wavering.

I thought I would provide the King James Version (KJV) and New Revised Standard Version (NRSV) of today's scripture.

Deuteronomy 17:19 (King James Version (KJV)

And it shall be with him, and he shall read therein all the days of his life: that he may learn to fear the LORD his God, to keep all the words of this law and these statutes, to do them:

Deuteronomy 17:19 New Revised Standard Version (NRSV)

It shall remain with him and he shall read in it all the days of his life, so that he may learn to fear the LORD his God, diligently observing all the words of this law and these statutes, I was introduced to, and grew in Christ, basically reading and understanding the KJV. In the church I joined in 2009, I listened to a minister teaching a bible study class suggest reading different versions of

God's Word for further clarity. I heard what he said, but I was like, I understand KJV....

Until a few years ago, when I was gifted with a Quest New International Version (NIV) study bible. At the time I thought, I do not need another bible (thinking re-gift). I have several, one in the car, one in my bathroom, and a couple stored in a closet. The funny thing is they were all KJV. As I started reading this new version (to me) I really liked the clarity and it encouraged me to read other versions. I still love and read the KJV, but I also read and compare other versions mostly using the NIV.

Another lesson for me ...that you cannot always stick to "I always do that; I can't do that because....; that's what I am used to doing, and I am not changing; that's what I have always done, and there is no other way to see or view it". I have learned, and continue to believe that is not true, for those of us in Christ. The Holy Spirit leads and guides us, and it is the Holy Spirit that we should rely on, believe in, and obey.

There are so many of God's blessings that we will not receive because we get stuck .....stuck on tradition; stuck on that's the way my parents did it; stuck on that's the way my old church did it; stuck on other people's version of what is right, so forth and so on...JUST STUCK. In His Word, God has provided many biblical examples where He gave guidance, and direction to his people and the other people around them had no understanding, and no idea what was about to happen, look at the stories of Noah, Job, Joseph, Moses, David, and most of all Jesus, just to name a few.....

Now going back to the Bible, I was gifted with, I thank God for it, it was and continues to be a blessing that I did not initially see. It provides me with more understanding of God's Word, taught me to be even more "OPEN"; to come out of my "COMFORT ZONE", and continue to grow according to God's Word, and His Holy Spirit.

Whether His messages come through reading different versions of His Word, just taking the "me" "you" out of the equation, or (as I heard in a song), it comes in a brown paper bag, just be, or learn to be obedient to the Spirit of God, I guarantee it will not stray you in the wrong direction. You may be taken out of your comfort zone, but when you realize why, you will leap for joy and praise God for being obedient. Something to give thought to......right?

Now may the Love of God be with you, the peace of Jesus maintain you and the Holy Spirit restrain you. In Jesus Name and For His Sake. Can I get an "AMEN" "AMEN" "AMEN

Journal

From the heart and Spirit of your Sister Algie Praying
that we, On Purpose, use God's Guidance.

Yes, there is an instruction book on how to live our lives.
It's called The Bible. It Starts from the beginning of time
until whatever your presence is. You will be amazed when
you pick it up. All the treasures of miracles and guidance
already pre-planned for us. Planned for you. God has
created you and designed you in His Likeness.

Psalm 25:5 AKJV

"Lead me in your truth and teach me: for you are the God
of my salvation; on you do I wait all the day."

Definition of (Plan) _ noun -a scheme or method of
acting, doing, proceeding, making, etc., developed in
advance: Plan refers to any method of thinking out, acts
and purposes beforehand: Designed made or done
intentionally; intended; planned.

So, God Created You on Purpose. If this is so, then that
means He has an outline for our lives. My suggestion is
that we go to The Bible, read it, study it, follow it, so we
can live productively. Not struggling every day,
wondering should I do this, or treat people like that.

Matthew 7: 7-11 ESV

"Ask, and it will be given to you; seek, and you will find; knock, and it will be opened to you. For everyone who asks receives, and the one who seeks finds, and to the one who knocks it will be opened. Or which one of you, if his son asks him for bread, will give him a stone? Or if he asks for a fish, will give him a serpent? If you then, who are evil, know how to give good gifts to your children, how much more will your Father who is in heaven give good things to those who ask him!

Every day I wake up and wonder what I should be doing. Am I following God's instruction? Am I living and showing His characteristics? I believe people should be able to see how Great God is through His followers. How we look and act. If we are happy, we should be smiling. When we are going through hard times, we should be hopeful and faithful. It is a responsibility, one that I am glad to uphold because when God rewards you it's like the sun coming out on a rainy day.

The light opens your mind and truth pours out. You ever feel something deep in your soul and you cannot hardly explain it. That is God, a sweet joy only He can give. A Peace received that you can only say Thank You Lord in your most quiet yet loud whisper. God and His answers for our lives are beyond all understanding. Yet it is open for us to receive. The answers were shown to me. Now I offer them to you.

Your Father loves you and wants your life easier. If you need a Bible let me know. Meanwhile I am praying your guidance in the Lord. Also, I am asking that you pray for my strength.

Journal

From the Heart and Spirit of Sister Badia A.

Good Monday Morning to you!

FOCUSED AND DRIVEN BY THE SPIRIT OF GOD

Rise and Shine! God, we give you all the glory and honor for you are worthy to be praised! In Jesus name, AMEN!

It was once said, somewhere in the most awesome book ever written (THE BIBLE) to "Set your minds on things that are above, not on things that are on earth" (Colossians 3:2 English ESV). Or, "Let your eyes look directly forward, and your gaze be straight before you" (Proverbs 4:25 ESV).

And, how about this one, "But seek first the kingdom of God and his righteousness, and all these things will be added to you" (Matthew 6:33 ESV). Because of these encouraging passages, we have a written blueprint, of what it takes to live Holy Spirit driven lives.

When I first accepted Christ as my Lord and Savior, I remember thinking what next. I was extremely excited about the change in my life. All I could think about is that

I wanted to know more about Jesus. I wanted to learn how to live like those around me. Those who, before me, made the decision to walk with the Lord. It became a priority for me to read and receive direction in my new life. I was focused, driven by the Spirit of God, yearning to receive more of Him.

Scripture says, "Therefore, there is now no condemnation for those who are in Christ Jesus, because through Christ Jesus the law of the Spirit who gives life has set you free from the law of sin and death. For what the law was powerless to do because it was weakened by the flesh, God did by sending his own Son in the likeness of sinful flesh to be a sin offering. And so, he condemned sin in the flesh, in order that the righteous requirement of the law might be fully met in us, who do not live according to the flesh but according to the Spirit.

Those who live according to the flesh have their minds set on what the flesh desires, but those who live in accordance with the Spirit have their minds set on what the Spirit

desires. The mind governed by the flesh is death, but the mind governed by the Spirit is life and peace" (Romans 8:1-6 NIV).

Thank God for Jesus! Thank God for loving us enough to incarnate himself in the flesh, to be a living sacrifice to the world. That is the spirit I want to follow. A selfless

Spirit that bore more than we could ever think and imagine. He did it all for us, so why not give our all to Him! Fully focused, Driven by the Spirit of God!!! AMEN!

Journal

From the Heart and Spirit of Sister Monica D.

Good Morning All!!

Lord we give thanks to You for this day. We thank you for waking us up and leading us on our way. Give us guidance throughout our day and let Your will be done. In Jesus name, Amen!

"When the Saints come marching in, oh how I want to be in that number, oh when the Saints come marching in!"

Will you be in that number?

Revelation 14:1-5 New International Version (NIV)

Then I looked, and there before me was the Lamb, standing on Mount Zion, and with him 144,000 who had his name and his Father's name written on their foreheads. And I heard a sound from heaven like the roar of rushing waters and like a loud peal of thunder. The sound I heard was like that of harpists playing their harps. And they sang a new song before the throne and before the four living creatures and the elders. No one could learn the song except the 144,000 who had been

redeemed from the earth. These are those who did not defile themselves with women, for they remained virgins. They follow the Lamb wherever he goes. They were purchased from among mankind and offered as first fruits to God and the Lamb. No lie was found in their mouths; they are blameless.

Are you saved? How is your relationship with God? Will you be in that number when Jesus comes to claim those who are righteous according to His will?

The word of God states that we will all fall short to His glory, meaning that no one is, was or will be perfect but our Lord, Jesus Christ. And it is ok that we are not perfect, but how much do you yearn to be righteous? Read, pray and meditate daily is a beginning to an everlasting relationship of learning and growing spiritually. Oh, how I want to be in the number, maybe not the 144,000 mentioned in this scripture, but among the righteous that will be chosen. Of course, there is more, but this is a great start. Begin today in the book of Genesis, that is where it all begins. The Book of

Revelations let us just say it is a beginning to an ending where we all hope to be ready.

Be Blessed, and Always Pray!!!

Journal

YOUR ASSIGNMENT: MY ROCK, MY RELATIONSHIP, MY RELIGION!!!

"Sister Juan" sharing a bit of HER(s)tory today, a few words, and a couple verses of scripture.

As I revealed to you last Thursday, I love my relationship with the Lord, Jesus Christ and the Holy Spirit. On Friday of last week, my SAFE sister Algie revealed that there are different areas of relationships (dating, marriage, church, friendship, etc.), but for a relationship to be biblical, it must be in accord with the teaching of Scripture. The word, "biblical" is an adjective and simply describes the relationship as one that meets the criterion of the Bible as it defines, describes, and delineates the principles that should characterize any relationship.

So, can you let your mind and spirit wander a bit, think about your relationship with Lord, Jesus Christ and the Holy Spirit...when it started; where you were, how you received it, and finally, how you are maintaining that relationship right now....

John 15:9-17 says "As the Father has loved me, so have I loved you. Now remain in my love. If you keep my commands, you will remain in my love, just as I have kept my Father's commands and remain in his love. I have told you this so that my joy may be in you and that your joy may be complete. My command is this: Love each other as I have loved you. Greater love has no one than this: to lay down one's life for one's friends. You are my friends if you do what I command. I no longer call you servants because a servant does not know his master's business. Instead, I have called you friends, for everything that I learned from my Father I have made known to you. You did not choose me, but I chose you and appointed you so that you might go and bear fruit— fruit that will last—and so that whatever you ask in my name the Father will give you. This is my command: Love each other."

Now may the Love of God be with you, the peace of Jesus maintain you and the Holy Spirit restrain you. In Jesus Name and For His Sake. Can I get an "AMEN" "AMEN" "AMEN

Journal

Hello Everyone, this is your Sister Algie, thanking God today for giving me the chance to Praise Him, and to ask for His Guidance in Encouraging you to cherish the Relationship He extends to us.

Psalm 104: 33-34

I will sing to the LORD all my life; I will sing praise to my God as long as I live. May my meditation be pleasing to him as I rejoice in the LORD.

Often, I ask myself how to do you make it through. When my life is off track and I do not know which way to turn, I reflect on my past, my illnesses, bills, marriage, children and all the rest of my needs that were taken care of. I am standing now because I trust my Father to help me through, or should I say carry me through. Now I must mention I did not stand in the middle of the floor and just ask. I prayed and listened to His instruction and got off my seat and put in the work.

James 2:14 New King James Version (NKJV)

Faith Without Works Is Dead
What does it profit, my brethren, if someone says he has faith but does not have works? Can faith save him?
But I will say this, there were times when I did not know what to do Or I might have chosen the wrong thing to do. So, I stayed still until I got my answer.

Psalms 46: 10 He says, "Be still, and know that I am God; I will be exalted among the nations, I will be exalted in the earth."

My Prayer: Dear Lord help me to be a better person to my friends and family. I am asking you for your strength in knowing where my help comes from. That it is from you. Sometimes I think I am to lean on myself, my family and friends. But Lord You are first. In the morning I should praise You first. The first in my earthly relationships. And, the first I thank before I go to bed at night.

Some might say why do you call on the Lord for everything. My answer is He is my Everything. Thank You Lord for loving me. Caring for me and never leaving or forsaking me in all my times and needs. In Jesus Name and for Your Sake Amen!

Journal

Good Monday Morning to you!

From the Heart and Spirit of Sister Badia A.

Rise and Shine! God, we give you all the glory *and honor for you are worthy to be praised! In Jesus name, AMEN!*

REVELATION, UNVEILED...

Did you know that, you are the key component in bringing God's prophesy to pass? It is you, who from the power of God, is chosen for a time such as this...... Let the Revelation be unveiled. It is time to work. Glory be to God for choosing us. Our assignment(s) takes grace, strength, knowledge, and wisdom. All these things are pieces of God's Holy Spirit to be demonstrated in difficult situations. It is time for the dream and or vision to take shape and be used in the place you are currently standing.

Ecclesiastes 3:3 (NIV) reads "There is a time for everything, and a season for every activity under the heavens." "So, I saw that there is nothing better for a person than to enjoy their work, because that is their lot. For who can bring them to see what will happen after

them" (Ecclesiastes 3: 22 NIV)? Thank God for His planned purpose for our lives. WE, thank Him for providing us the tools of transformation. And lastly, we thank Him for providing us the time for it all to come to pass.

When I think about my purpose and God's timing. Thoughts of what it took for me to get to this place in my assignment becomes clear. I noticed that through it all, nothing would be completed, had I not made the decision to SHOW UP! "My presence is needed", is the thought that constantly run through my mind, during my time of mediation. I am an important instrument in God's kingdom. What He equipped me with is a tool of strength, from the trials, He victoriously brought me through. Bless be to God for revealing to me who I am to Him, and His kingdom. I learned that my existence is needed for His plan through my life. So, I praise the Lord for my trials, as I count them all as stepping stools to get me where I need to be, in Him. God's revelation was unveiled when I recognized my worth. I am worthy to be used to the highest capacity in which our father chooses to use me.... And, so are you!

Encouragement

Allow the Lord to minister to your purpose. If He showed you who you are? Trust, that He can equip, and allow

Him to use you. It is time for His revelation to be unveiled. All you must do is SHOW UP!

Journal

From the Heart and Spirit of Sister Monica D.

Good Morning Everyone!

Thank You Lord for this glorious day! We may not know what is ahead of us Lord, but we know that You will reveal Your glory in all that we receive throughout this day. In Jesus name, Amen!!

I believe a lot of people are wandering and are wasting a lot of time to what it is they already know. The sad part of it is, most people know and have realized that if they open their heart and choose to believe that there is a Higher Power who is God. Then that takes away their own greatness. You see greater is He that is in me than he who is in the world. As a child of God, I can do all things through Christ that strengthens me. But in the world alone, I am nothing. God reveals Himself throughout His word, and through His Son Jesus and the Holy Spirit. Get to know Christ for yourself and begin to live for purpose. In so many scriptures, He is revealed. And the way God reveals Himself throughout and in His word, He teaches through guidance, instruction and vision of His plan to His righteousness for us. Just for us! Hallelujah, Glory be to God! Why not follow Christ?

Revelations 1:8 (NLT)

"I am the one who is, who always was, and who is still to come—the Almighty One." It is then revealed, who He is.

Be Blessed and Always Pray!

Journal

From the heart and spirit of Sister Juan sharing biblical scriptures and HER(s)tory without wavering.

Again, thanking GOD for a great getting up morning - I have the love of Jesus in my HEART (singing voice) - I am my beloved's--my beloved is mine. Love this verse from Solomon Song of Songs 6:3, (brought a ring with the same message) Mine all mine, JESUS I know He is mine (LOUD singing voice)

Psalm 103:1-5 (NIV) "Praise the Lord, my soul; all my inmost being, praise his holy name. Praise the Lord, my soul, and forget not all his benefits— who forgives all your sins and heals all your diseases, who redeems your life from the pit and crowns you with love and compassion, who satisfies your desires with good things so that your youth is renewed like the eagle's...." I love these verses of Psalm 103; they have become a part of my prayer life every day. I am reminded of the moment the Lord give me these words many years ago. The Holy Spirit told me to recite it before I prayed in private, and in public, and I have been obedient to do just that.

The funny thing is for a long time I did not read the full scripture, just verses 1-5. THEN, one day I read and studied the whole psalm, (which I recommend to you today) it opened my eyes and soul even more. I then fully understood why the Holy Spirit instructed me to take a hold of it in my prayer life.

It encompasses so much encouragement, and further confirms the comfort and truth of God's Word, which is beautifully manifested in a person who has accepted Jesus Christ as their Savior, and illustrates their steadfast love and determination to serve God, by being obedient to the Holy Spirit. And may I end with "Bless the Lord O my soul!!!!! How are you blessing the Lord today......?

Now may the Love of God be with you, the peace of Jesus maintain you and the Holy Spirit restrain you. In Jesus Name and For His Sake. Can I get an "AMEN" "AMEN" "AMEN

Journal

| |
| |
| |
| |
| |
| |
| |
| |
| |
| |
| |
| |

This is another day that the Lord has made. We might as well wake up and enjoy it!

Hello my sisters and brothers, this is your Sister Algie, here to encourage you to keep the relationships that are important to you.

You know things can happen in the blink of an eye. Time goes by, children grow up, parents get older and so will you. Lake a shift in the Universe things will change. Birth, Happiness, Death, Sadness. I always say do not miss your opportunities and live your life On Purpose!

Hug somebody today. Talk to them and let them know you care. Have anyone ever told you they do not hug. Reeeealy, I cannot imagine never getting or giving a hug. Well, let me tell you about Someone, that without physically touching you, gives the best hugs. God! You can just talk to him and He can fill your Heart with such joy and take away pain! God can do it. He wants to have a relationship with you, a personal relationship. And, supply all your needs.

One thing that will never change is how much God loves you. He loves us now and forever more. He is our Father and He always wants the best for us. So take all you needs to Him. And on you way Praise Him as if you have already received your answers, your blessings.

Luke 11:9 "So I say to you: Ask and it will be given to you; seek and you will find; knock and the door will be opened to you.

Luke 10:27 He answered, "Love the Lord you God with all your heart and with all our soul and with all our strength and with all your mind" and "Love you neighbor as yourself"...

160

Reading these scriptures blessed me. I pray they blessed you as well.

Journal